What's My Value Add?

By

Andrew R. Flagg

aka Andrew Jackson Wilson

"One will soon realize that over time that their careful and continuous introspection and application of one's curiosity and discovery of what is within you is the beauty of a joyful life just waiting to happen."

*Author Unknown *ahem* yours truly, Andy*

Send Suggestions to:

Andrew R Flagg c/o Mountain Publishing
490 E 8th St, Suite 200-C, Reno Nevada USA 89512
Calling Internationally +1 011 775-525-2830

Email to: WhatsMyValueAdd@MountainPublishing.org

Twitter Handles: @MntnPublishing

Facebook: http://facebook.com/MountainPublishing

Website: http://www.MountainPublishing.org

PURPOSE & INTENT

What's My Value Add is not your everyday kind of read. It will help you better understand your current situation and balance that against what you have in your current life in what I call a "toolkit" or "toolbox". Your self-analysis will help you build, rebuild and expand to improve your "toolbox".

What's My Value Add can also be a guide and suggestion for you to look at your life as a whole. From the beginning to the ending, looking forward or in reverse on how you can achieve that which you desire and are destined to achieve and be. While this is not a comprehensive approach and long winded, it gives you my approach to a simple and happy life. My life has been more perfect than flawed.

This book is going to be a fast exploration of your value add. It might take you a lifetime to figure it out, or like me, had it figured out a few times, over and over, and over again.

This short book does not represent all forms of thinkers and believers. Some might read this and get it right away, and others might take a little longer, and some might never get it. C'est la vie.

DISCLAIMER, TERMS & AGREEMENTS

All the names and places in this book are fictitious except the author. The reason why we did this is to protect everyone at the same time. Though some might resemble real names and places, they are not.

The due diligence it took to research this book and write it under free and protected speech was done to the best of one's abilities, counsel, and resources.

Anyone who purchases, possesses or receives this book by any means, your acceptance of this book you agree to not do, act or file anything against anyone for things like slander, libel, invasion of privacy, copyright or trademark or other legal challenges; however, one is allowed the opportunity to submit revisions and improvements for the next revision as new and more interesting concepts and feedback are explored.

FIRST IMPRESSIONS & REVIEWS

"WMVA is thought provoking and an eye-opener. I thought I had heard it all until I skimmed through a few of the pages and picked up a few tidbits and spin on how I see things and coach my clients." ~ Trevor J. – Life Coach and Counselor – New Mexico

"Mr. Flagg definitely captures a different aspect on the approach to life sort of ass backwards. He does not mince words and pretty much tells you how things are and how they can be at the same time. Even I procrastinate like him to a fault, but then realize we all have an end game we are not yet aware of and needs to be planned and played out." ~ Karen Michaels. – Director of the Center for Aging, Norfolk VA

"Beyond a preponderance of thought, What's My Value Add is definitely something to read in the early morning or evening when you have time to ponder your beginning and ending of the day and your life. Did you achieve what you expected? What are your plans for the day?" Victoria Elizabeth Grant, Atchison Law Group, Denver, CO.

FORWARD BY DREW JACKSON

This is one of the fastest approaches I have seen in one's overall life style analysis in years. I have written dozens of books on psychology and introspection and read hundreds of self-improvement books, life coaching guides and attended many seminars on leadership and attaining excellence, yet this one approach to reverse analysis is quite astounding.

Andrew's approach and coverage of concepts reminds me of one of my greatest experiences in a venue in Seattle Washington some 30 years ago, it was a pursuit of excellent series that was well organized just like Andrew's approach in this book. Enjoy the read. It's worth the time.

ANDREW'S DEDICATION

This book has been written and dedicated to my wife, mentors and friends. My wife gets special consideration considering all that she has experienced and offers in my life and the lives of others.

Thank you to all the mentors I have been helped by whether or not they knew they were a mentor to me or not.

One will soon realize that over time that their careful and continuous introspection and application of one's curiosity and discovery of what is within you is the beauty of a joyful life just waiting to happen.

ANDREW'S ACKNOWLEDGMENTS

I am deeply grateful for my family and friends who have stood by me through all the good and bad times. I am equally thankful for my team of reviewers and editors, and legal helpers who have taken the time out of their busy schedule to provide their wisdom and feedback.

My journey from Oregon throughout America where I have been blessed and challenged throughout my life could not be done without the help of so many. I love my Dad & Mom who have passed, and I love my remaining living family members, and continue to believe in their success, health and happiness. This book might help those in need beyond my own dreams, hopes, wishes and life.

REVIEWS

Be sure to follow up and write a review, even if you only read a few pages, picked up the book, put it down, and then shelved it. To acknowledge any part of it is a contribution to your effort and the efforts of others. Good, bad or indifferent; your feedback is just that, and important part of the improvement process. Rule of Three. Pick up the book, flip through it and scan it for interesting things and digest it, and then put the book down and submit some comments. Easy peazy, lemon squeezy.

TABLE OF CONTENTS

Chapter 1 – Prologue

In the beginning, you are a drop of water.

You are hanging in the air above a large pool of water.

The pool of water is the world and life as you see it and not as you will begin to know it once you become part of it.

What will be your value add to that pool of water?

Will you make a difference and if so, how?

It's not a race or a competition to figure it out.

Enjoy the fact that you have been on a path for a very long time, your path, that no one else can or will walk.

You will never be alone.

Your soul will be your friend, and your heart will hold and protect your happiness, and your mind will claim and carry and your memories of your travels and adventures.

In the end, you are a drop, just a drop of water.

Let the water cycle of your life begin, flow, and never end.

Note to Reader: Not everyone likes a Prologue. I do. Awkward, I know.

Ps. I wanted chapter 2 to be chapter 1, but I wanted the Prologue to be in the Table of Contents. Sorry typesetters and publishers. Life goes on.

About this book, thoughts from a fellow published writer

Before we get started and what you should know about this book, a great published writer a few months looked at my first book that I had written as a ghost writer called "The Appellant" and asked a single question. This applies to how this book comes to you as well.

He asked me, "How many errors are in your book?"

I replied, "A lot!"

He said, "That's great. Now I know it's going to be a great read. If there were no errors your story would be boring."

I smiled and smirked.

We both agreed that a perfect book is boring, and one filled with a few errors can be interesting to the reader because it stops them for a second to re-read the sentences and paragraph, and go back and forth in the book to get the meaning, and possibly find new meaning in what they just read.

I added to his thoughts, and shared that even though I am a spelling bee freak, a spelling error will stop a person. Maybe that is a good reason to have an imperfect sentence or word or two. It demonstrates imperfection and vulnerability. A perfect sentence a reader will glaze over. We both parted with a smile and agreeing nod.

…more to come…

Sorry about the segue. On with "What's My Value Add" – Chapter 2.

Chapter 2 – Spatial Orientation

Spatial orientation and or better yet spatial proximity might seem like a mouth full, yet they are not. Both have to do with you and the rest of what is around you, mainly the world and larger yet, the infinite universe. That seemed like a long yucky paragraph. Well, get over it. There is more to come. *Grin.*

Have you ever looked at something and visualized nearly accurately what was on the other side? Have you ever attempted to send, cast, or project your vision and ability to see and view things such that you can look at something and see it from all sides from all angles simultaneously, and maneuver around it with ease? What about seeing something move through time, from birth, aging, and decay.

Do you usually know which way is north without a compass? Can you pretty much guess what is going to happen after you do something and look down the road of life and know that in a day, week, month or year what is going to happen next? Even easier, basically, do you know what's going around you if you are or are not the center of focus? Right now, all the time, from time to time.

Spatial orientation and proximity awareness basically answer those questions as being self-evident and true if you are one of the lucky who can do that.

Get out of first gear and shift into third gear or overdrive. Tell yourself that. Have you ever worked with people who could never seem to get out of first gear? Mind you, we do need those people around. They are called sustainers and maintainers. While you are maybe a mover and shaker, I would like to call yourself a challenger and changer.

Accelerate and Fast Forward your vision and conceptual skills such that you can step outside yourself and look back at yourself from near or far. Project your mind's eye to observer yourself within your immediate vicinity, and your area, your town, city, then over the horizon and around the planet, and beyond. Is this your imagination at work, or are you really able to see beyond with your mind at any given moment by choice and focus?

Do you dream? Do you remember your dreams? Are your dreams in color or black and white? Some might seem like this is using your imagination. Is it really? Are you sure?

Have you ever heard of Deja-vu? Have you noticed yourself doing or seeing something that you believed you had already done before? How often has this happened? Are you so aware and tuned in that you know what happens next?

Are you truly aware of your surroundings? When you step back and start to notice everything using your five senses, even the sense beyond your first five senses, you start to notice things that might seem strange but are rather normal if you are "tuned in".

Finally, can you look down and at yourself and see everything instantly? Can you sketch that view on a piece of paper quickly and then fill in all the details? Uncanny is it not? What is that called?

...more to come...

Chapter 3 – Invert Your Approach

Living life right side up seems like normal, but really its more fun to turn things around and over and look at things upside down.

What are some topics that this might apply?

Communication and Feedback, Leadership and Management, Education and Training, and so on and so forth. In Chapter 4 we will expand on those but let's explore some thinking in how you begin to invert your approach. How do you get from here to there? From being a normal thinker to one of a hybrid and abstract thinker.

Have you ever watched somebody and how they approached something and you realized they were working harder than they should be? They take 5 steps where you would take 2 steps. They would go back and forth a few times and meander around a solution whereas you would go straight towards solution.

If you can take something apart, you can put it back together, usually. I learned how have a mechanical aptitude as a child by taking apart a bicycle I found in a ditch and restored it in my Dad's shop. Take it completely apart, repaint it, lube it, fix the gears, spokes and brakes and cables, and voila. That ended up being the start of a new life as a desire to tinker with all things. Take apart a toaster and put it back together.

Are you a risk taker? Calculated risks are a sign of a great leader and manager and person in general. In addition, most leaders make mistakes and learn from them and apply that experience to the next situation. Leaders are not like everyone else. If everyone jumps off a cliff, do you? Probably not.

When you walk into a room, do you scan the perimeter, scan the crowd, take note of the windows and doors, and take a quick snapshot of things that are normal and things that are out of place. You just don't walk in and say you are there and here. You calculate your entrance, your exit. You do a quick analysis of colors, floor plan, power, lighting, water, windows, ceiling, things on wheels, tall people, short people, those that are armed, those that are elderly. All of these things add up to your ability to keep track of your space no matter what happens.

Do you ever just drive down a road that says Dead End or No Outlet only to find there is a way through? Do you take note and remember all the alleys and backyards, roofs, gates? What about vehicles parked in your neighborhood that just don't match or below. If they are parked for an hour, a day, a week.

Do you have kids? How do you talk to them? Do you ask them more questions than making statements? Do you have quality time with them and learn how to be a friend with them as well as a parent? Do you notice when they are watching you and analyzing you and taking mental notes of your behavior. Do you role play with them with situations like "what if" this or that. Treating your kids like adults before they are ready is important. Look at your life through your kids eyes. Going backwards in life, make sure they know you are looking forwards and backwards through your life, their life and the lives of others and how it does matter to consider all things relevant.

On another note, I have a saying, "If you lie to me, then I must have done something to make you want to." Usually its all about rejection. No one lies to be accepted, unless your childhood required it, but as an adult, it is usually is fear of rejection. Therefore, when someone lies to me, or I feel tempted to lie, then either I avoid the situation at all costs to avoid lying or tell someone and ask them, "If you want to ask a hard question of me, be prepared for a hard answer." Better yet, just tell the person, you would prefer not to lie and let them know for some reason you are being put in a position to lie, and you don't want to.

Are there any other secrets about inverting your approach I can share? Maybe. Not yet. Let me get this edition out the door and then come and back and fill in the blanks with feedback on what we have already covered.

...more to come...

On to chapter 4.

Chapter 4 – The Strategy of Approach

A strategy of approach is how one begins to take on something that needs guile and keen senses. This could be almost anything you do if you think hard enough. Others might be too lassie-faire to think about every move they make.

In the previous chapter we explored just lines of thinking in how to invert your approach. Everyone has experiences as good, great, better and bad, and in approaching something, sometime inverting your thinking and belief system sometimes just works.

For some like me, rushing into a situation is a bad idea anywhere and anytime. Using my instincts first and foremost, added by experiences and wisdom, along with a dash of luck and timing, one can succeed time after time.

This leads to those topics in the previous chapter, we wanted to discuss after we broached up all the ways one warms up to a strategy. Let's begin.

Communication and Feedback.

Why is the most important thing you have to say come always at the end? When it's all said and done, you have this conclusion. Why not have the epiphany of presenting the end at the beginning? What about asking the last question first, and if so how does that change things?

Movies sometimes show the end, and work backwards or forwards to return to how the end was achieved. That's mysterious and entertaining at the same time.

What about when you go to a job interview and you are asked a series of questions about why you are a good fit for the position and company, and then you get to ask your questions. What is your first or last question? You better have a few good ones and make sure they are not threatening. After all, you have carefully planned ahead and learned all about the company from trade news, corporate filings, the whisper word on the street, stockholder and analyst opinions.

You don't want to pry and you want to sound intelligent, yet the last question should be, "Are there any questions I should have asked that I have not yet asked?" The look from the other side of the table might come as a smile. Your interviewer might be caught off guard or pleasantly surprised. It might seem odd. You might get another interview after listening to their take on your question.

Leadership and Management.

So how do you approach things? Top to bottom, bottom to top, or 360 degrees around?

This is an interesting question for those in corporate America or in organizations that have high employee involvement to some degree. Are you in management, yes or no. I don't care if the word "manager" is in your job title. Only a real manager is one who can hire and fire, bind or dissolve contracts.

Any other manager is purely fictional in terms of active management. Yes, Yes, while there are vendor managers, project managers and so on, these are managers of things, not people, and have no direct reporting or responsibility to subordinates. Even dotted line reporting is not really people management. You might be able to offer input on another's review for promotion, compensation, but you have no direct say on other than providing feedback.

If you are in management, great. If you are not, I suggest getting there before the age of 45 if you planning on having a good livelihood in your years between 45 and 70. In this day and age, if you are in staff after age 45, you might not be able to defend yourself when organizations have layoffs and mergers, and staff reductions in force.

Remember, leadership and management in combination with staff is not about a democracy. Everyone does get a vote, yet the key is that sometimes your vote is just "noted".

Leaders will decide one way one day based on the information they have, and the next day change it based on new information. That's leading. Staff and other leaders and managers get use to that.

I was once told that I am the only person they have heard the word "No" from so many times. I replied, "You just have not told me enough for me to say Yes. No does not mean forever, it just means for today." That leadings and being open and specific at the same time.

Before we change subjects, remember this; the difference between a great CEO and a bad one regardless if they have an Ivy League degree or not is whether they care more about the bottom dollar and shareholders and how they are viewed versus how they are balanced and passionate about the team they guide to deliver products and services for a profit with due care, diligence and ethics. If you can do both, great! If not yet, keep trying. If the CEO goes into a lavatory or bathroom that is being cleaned, and knows the janitor (male or female) by name and has a polite and meaningful conversation, that shows you something positive about the leader's integrity and wisdom.

Education & Training.

College – Do you know what you want a degree in?

Some colleges gradually get you started with general studies and other things that are not core to your degree. It's a way of easing you into college life for fun. I believe that is a mistake unless you are there for the fun only for a while. Eventually you will have to get serious and graduate or not. College does not have to be hard, but it needs to be focused and aggressively focused on your outcomes.

If you start your day 1 as if you are counting backwards, you want that degree in your hand now so you can do what you believe and dream of being and doing as a profession. For some a four-year degree might take five or six years, and for some others, longer. I have seen and become familiar with career college students. Hopefully that is not your path.

The best hope and chance you have is to get a degree or series of degrees where the market place is in demand of you now and then, and your net worth increases over time at a pace that you can handle.

Here is the trick – if you know what you want and don't want to waste your time, see if you can invert your curriculum and take your junior and senior level courses in your freshman and sophomore years. If so, take those specific core courses first and either pass with flying colors or drop out quickly so you know it's not for you. Then, if you like your degree and studies so much and you know there is application in the real world, then know that going into your junior and senior years. Your junior and senior projects will be focused on your advanced courses and to fill in the gap to get the credits you need to graduate can be fun electives and general studies.

Overarching Outlook on Life.

Remember to be honest with yourself in your strategy and approach and do what pushes you and encourages you yet at the same time keeps you out of the rat race. For the rest of your life it might seem you are being competitive with everyone around you, yet, like in golf, you are really just competing with yourself and trying to better and improve yourself with each and every step in your game of life.

What you will find attractive and challenging might not be the same for others. You will see for yourself what makes your life happy and fulfilled. Stick to your guns and your strategy, and by all means, pick up a mentor and someone you look up to that is not necessarily perfect but is hard working and ethical and demands more of themselves than they demand of you. Let their actions be an example to you of how much you want to be like them.

Remember, this is your life, your strategy might be a multitude and combination of other strategies from others, along with a little imagination and creativity from yourself at the same time.

…more to come…

Chapter 5 – Analyze Keenly

The process of analyzing anything can be both a science and art. While some of us are built to analyze others are not. Ironically, many people can be narrowly focused by design while others are broadly focused. That difference is what makes each of us unique in our skills and abilities to do certain things to a certain degree.

Have you have heard of microscopic and macroscopic thinking? The ability to look into all areas of life or look at something from 20,000 feet down to 20 feet. Can you do both? What about one more than the other? If you can, great. If not, apply yourself and open up to the time when someone says you are looking at things to closely or you are not looking at things close enough. That rhetoric drives me crazy but alas, when I was younger, maybe so. By the time you hit 50 years old, you better have that down to both an art and science. Moving on…

Peripheral Vision – Do you have it?

Do not get tunnel vision. Have you ever watched someone and looked at where their eyes were looking? As a support professional and trainer, I always ask a person a question sometimes rhetorically and look at where their eyes go in terms of finding an answer. Most times folks have tunnel vision and are not looking around to find solutions.

What about analyzing a book?

If there is an index, count the number of pages that a word is referenced for weighting to see what the indexer or author leaned on in terms of word choice and focus of writing. I do it regularly to see where the indexer or author found the most weight and focus of their subject. It might reveal something interesting to your subject of study.

On a side note, do you enjoy wandering around in libraries, or collecting encyclopedias for fun? Oddly, when I was a child, I had an encyclopedia set in my bedroom, a hand me down from someone to the family, and when I got grounded to my bedroom for ½ a day, that is what I would do, read the encyclopedias. Now I collect encyclopedia sets, the ones that are affordable and read those when I need a bathroom break. Odd, but true. On with more interesting tidbits and trivia to unwrap and unfold.

What about chaos?

Have you ever known when chaos exists, there are those that thrive and those that die? Which are you? Do you improve and perform well under stress or are you basically someone who prefers zero stress and no tolerance for pain?

I go in and out of maintenance mode to development mode. Where I will work hard for 2-3 months, and then settle down and coast for a month, and then repeat. This is about balancing your energy and contemplating your efforts to make sure you are progressing. Also, working under the radar to get something done is sometimes hard to do. Most people are so wrapped up in their own life that they don't notice the subtle and slight changes in you that compile and compound over time to become something rather large and different.

Your life might look like chaos to others, but it's your chaos. Their life might look chaos to you, but we each own and live through our own baggage and drama. I personally don't like drama. It's like gossip, it's just not healthy. Stop the Chaos! Mind your own business, create something cool over and over, and share your little wins.

What about focus and be tuned in?

Are you occasionally zoned out and seeing the world differently than others? Are you always focused and tuned in? I know some that I interact with who are "so busy". Busy-busy-busy, yet I don't hear the words productive. Being busy is easy. Being productive is a different type of focus. Is it just semantics or is it that they are too busy to notice or care about you, until they need something from you.

Where do you draft, keep and bring life to your ideas?

I call it a folder. I will tell you more about this folder and how it applies to other folders further down in the book.

For now, analyzing keenly is about staying focused on your ideas and inventions and occasionally adding more as they come to mind. Many inventions will just remain ideas until you reanalyze them keenly prototype and bring them to life and to the public at large. Some will be great hits and others will be absolute flops. In either outcome, your focus and being tuned into your innovation is of the utmost important.

A friend of mine sometimes is so focused he just ignores me not because he means to, he just works so deeply in his own world and bubble and doesn't keep his eyes and ears turned in my direction unless I scream or send him condolences of his untimely death. Then he perks up and apologizes. Now that is focus on his part. Ironically, when he emails me or contacts me, I pick up and reply. It's always a pleasure to listen to and help a dear and life-long friend.

…more to come…

Chapter 6 – By the Numbers

Did I do well in math classes? Nope! I got solid Bs. It was not until I read a book about getting straight A's that I was able to go from a 3.3 GPA to a constant 3.7 GPA or higher. This all had to about numbers. The number of times I rewrote my notes from class, the number of times I re-did the homework assignments.

Numbers are a very interesting creation. In work, finance, engineering, those funny things like 1, 2, 3, and other integers and fractions like 1/8th, 5/8th, 11/12th are all interesting. Even Greek and Roman letters, and all sorts of symbols and even Pi / π are interesting. Do you know your character maps and ASCII codes, or HTML codes? While all of these have application somewhere, the basics matter.

What is your favorite number? Favorite letter? Where does your favorite number come from? There is a story I am sure.

Let's explore a few types of numbers that you might have focused on or had on your athletic sport shirt at some point in your life. For me, the #7 was always my favorite, yet the number 3 has a special meaning as well.

Let's get started.

3 – Why is this number special?

There are many ways to look at the number 3. Three.

1+1+1 = 3

3/3 = 1

$$3/1 = 3$$

For the number 3, The Trinity might come to mind for some.

The Rule of Three also is a passion of mine. Look that one up and you will see there is some science behind it, and some colloquial conversation about it as well.

Let's cover a few ideas of how the number three works in real practice.

One example I have always referred to in projects and writing proposals, the Rule of 3 comes to the document. Page 1, executive page, and Page 2 the Summary, and Page 3 the raw data. Page 1 can be worth $1 to $100 million. It does not matter. If you can't get your point across in one page, the Executive page, then you have failed as a leader.

Another example of the Rule of 3 is how you write a book, probably a fiction book without the usage of chapters: Introduction, Body, and Conclusion. That one is easy to explain.

Bonus Round: here is a trick approach to the number three.

When you have numbers and situations where it seems like you only have two choices, like in or out, binary 0 or 1, black or white, up versus down, left versus right – there is a "three" in there, and it's called the transition. From going from either state or situation, you will be in a third situation, the transition and that can be your 1, 2 and 3. Don't forget, that the rule of 3 can apply to everything. Most people can remember three things, on three fingers. Make it five things, no so easy. Make it ten, even harder. Make it one, well, there is no fun in just one rule, well, maybe the Golden Rule is a good one.

Tricky, I know, but it's real. Don't let your children play with you on that thought and line of thinking. You could be right or wrong, and somewhere in between? There is a lot of grey or is it gray in between right and wrong.

7 – Is the number Seven special?

Besides being my favorite number and lucky number in Little League Baseball as a child, it has some other significance. It could be God's number, so they say.

Seven seems like a good number when you are child, though three was my lucky age, or each and every age that was a prime number. For me, 3, 27, 31, 41, 51, all had some significance.

Pi / π 3.1416~

This is an interesting number. If you do mathematics or program computers for any reason, this number will cross your path a few times in life. It can be used for so many things. Ironically, one thing it can be used for is cryptography and obfuscation. If you don't know by now, check it out online.

$ the Dollar Sign

If you want to have fun with your passwords in life of surfing the Internet, be sure to prepend your existing passwords with a few dollar signs. Even a single dollar sign can cause havoc for a system administrator. Some system systems, it is disallowed. In programming it can be useful to know when and how to use a dollar sign.

% Percentage Sign

This one is a little more interesting than the dollar sign. It in many ways is just like the dollar sign, but has an interesting use and methodology to its madness. One of the keys to riches in wisdom is to know your percentages by heart; from 0% to 100%, and ironically there are some markers in between that become useful. 49% versus 51%, 33% versus 66%, and 99.999% percent. Knowing 10% of a base multiplied to the right increment can be of fast use in math.

Are there Special Number Arrangements? Yes.

There are a few and could be many. Can you name a few? 80/20? 95/5? Fibonacci sequence is interesting but I won't go there this time around.

Can you look at a pattern of numbers and letters, a scatter gram or a big canvas of numbers and see patterns. Are you great at word search? Are you color blind?

Do you dream in color or black and white?

Do numbers and their special arrangements that you can discern allow you to dream you speak a foreign language like French or play the piano perfectly for years, and awake and be able to speak French perfectly for hours, or play the piano perfectly for hours?

There is more to numbers than you might realize. The best way to look at numbers is to see them easy to master, not hard.

What is my version of the 80/20 rule?

The Pareto Rule. Where 20% of the people do 80% of the real work and vice-versa 80% of the people do 20% of the work. I get that when I worked at a major software manufacturing company up Redmond Washington. When you have 20% of the team doing 80% of the work, the real work, then you have 80% overhead but then again, you need that. You have movers and shakers, the 20% and then you have maintainers and sustainers, that's the 80%. You need both, sort of, even though stock and shareholders prefer to eliminate that 80% overall since that sometimes is a suck on the company as a whole. I get it. That again is another approach to looking at life this number relationship.

What my version of the 95/5 rule?

Then there is another way of thinking that I came up with called the 95/5 rule based on a series of other approaches using it. Do you know what that is? It means, at 95% of the project completed, and 5% remaining, call the project complete. The remaining 5% move off the table and to another team, the A team and have them complete the 5% of the project.

Also, in business the 95/5 represents your income. 5% of your customers provide 95% of your income. Therefore, while the 95% are important, the 5% are your major clients and sources of income. Adjust your priorities and balance your work and focus accordingly.

What's your value add if you know math? Major!!!!

Up next, just try something with your new thinking on numbers. Do you calculate and tabulate? If you try something do you set metrics to measure progress? If not, no time like the present.

…more to come…

Chapter 7 – Just Try Something

I wanted to call this chapter "Conceptualize, Invent & Prototype" but that seemed to long and too analytical. Really, I just want you to understand that you need to try your ideas, sort of all the time. That folder of innovation and ideas is very important.

Awhile back, I read a note by someone who I considered was somewhat conceited and shared to me not to rock the boat. Ergo, don't try something and change for the better. I believe it was more about their control over me and not about our mutual growth, let alone my actual growth and success. No one around you likes you to change if it means they don't get to use you like they did before, but if you don't change you won't improve yourself. Drop the energy suckers and drama creators from your life.

So, with that in mind, rock the boat or don't rock the boat, but then again, it's your boat, right? I recall a quote where the sea is so great and your boat is so small, and then again, a boat that never leaves the safety of the harbor will never know the sea.

With all that wisdom about trying something, would you just sit down with an 8.5" x 11 piece of paper and capture and begin your thoughts and put that paper in a folder. Date that piece of paper and title that folder something you like to call *your folder of ideas, innovations,* etc. Remember that folder of ideas I wanted you to start. This is it. Try something without costing a lot of money. Be curious. Be a self-starter. Some employers like that in a person, a future leader or manager.

If you recall, all of your life you do things out of necessity and often times not just for yourself, but for the acceptance by others. That sort of has to stop as you get older and wiser. When you start coming up with ideas, what's the first thing you should do? Don't forget them. Don't procrastinate and forget them. The answer is: write them down.

So, to reiterate, get a folder, with a cool color, a log book or journal and call it "Invention Folder, Ideas, Innovation" and put that on your desk just close enough to open it and flip through it as the years go by in your life. When you have an idea, grab an 8.5" x 11" blank piece of paper, and sketch down your thoughts and ideas, give some attribution if necessary, write the date/time and place, and your signature and name, initials. Put a heading or title on it too, even if it is a half-baked idea. Don't forget to have someone your trust to sign it to or initial it to witness it. They don't have to understand it other than it was your idea and they can recall what you called it if the need arises.

Note to the reader about folder color: When I used to lead and manage large and expensive projects at a major corporation, sometimes projects costing $25,000 to $1 million that needed a signature from higher authority, the color of the folder was appropriate to the value of the project. Any non-standard colored manila folder would do, and not your ordinary manila folder color. Therefore, I could walk by any of my leaders and managers offices and see if my folder and project was on their desk waiting to be reviewed and signed. Sometimes, I would say good morning to one of them and mention something about the project and they would take a moment and try to find it and I would say, oh, it's the colored folder, and they would reach over and find it sign it and pass it back to me or have me pass to the next in line. Brilliant or not? Folders and Colors. Remember. Folders and Colors

…more to come….

Chapter 8 – Staying Relevant

So, what do you do to stay relevant. I promise to give you the answer first and then explain. Staying relevant is a big issue.

What's the trick? Going by the rule of 3 restrictions(s):

1. Keep up with your surroundings and look beyond your toolbox contents and bring in concepts and solutions from afar. Merchant traders from the past would bring new ideas, products and concepts from their travels.
2. Keep your home, office, and all living and working space free of clutter. Have a creative space that even your wife and family know as your space to invent, explore and create. Don't collect baggage, stuff, and drama.
3. Apply what you learn as quickly as possible, and if you can't be sure to save it in a space (your folder) of ideas. Document your ideas and improvements and schedule to apply them sooner than later. It's not about procrastination which has a way into seeming like slow wisdom but it works. Recall using your instincts and not others opinions. Remember, the Rule of 3.

Continuing, as you get older you tend to become less attractive to everyone. You have opinions, ideas, you look different, and you are ½ as fast as the person who is half your age.

This age dilemma has been going on forever. The young push out the old in an aging society where the young don't care for the old, and the society of "me" in the Western culture is everywhere.

Employers want you to be relevant but only at great cost and tragedy. Is there room for an aging baby boomer society? The cost of living and aging people's choices of where and how they want to live indicates a cost which they cannot necessarily support.

Unless you are a targeted demographic where the system supports your kind, there is reverse discrimination everywhere. Ironically, the checkboxes for age, gender, veteran status is just wrong. Token hires I believed were in the past. At my first job, I was told pay for performance, and seniority is not a consideration. Big lie there. I had to buck the system and use the system's rules against itself in order to move up the so-called ladder and do great things.

Even HR is against you staying relevant over the long term. Usually it is due to a lack of resources, lack of professional development planning and execution nerves, and bias towards just being human and judging others without real merit. A few human resource individuals typically create most of the hidden chaos from the inside and the outside. They just won't admit it and let alone fix it until there is a grand class action suit against their employer.

Have you ever heard from someone that were told you were thinking too much? That's a good thing, right? Not so. Being smart can be a turn off and though within yourself you might be quite brilliant; the rest of the world might be turned off by it. There is a significant difference between being confident versus arrogant. Both come off to some people as bad, but it depends on where they are coming from, and not necessarily about you.

To overcome growing dissention and rejection as being the smart one, the quick answer is to remain intelligent on the inside and look unintelligent and normal on the outside. Yeah, right?! This does not mean dress poorly, just moderately. Some of us have great looks and some of us are not so blessed. Now, don't go off and become hipster either. I worked in a library and looked normal, yet really inside I was a card catalog and index of all things seen and known. Research was natural. The idea is that a librarian with glasses on by day is not necessarily the same after the day is done, or however that saying goes.

The key is to be aware of all the knowledge you have available and capture (screen shot by blinking your eyes), tag and sort, and quick store the information and process it constantly. Don't let me forget to tell you how to archive and purge your active database and keep an archived index and long-term storage ready for retrieval. Being relevant is being able to access your entire life's knowledge base at the right time for the right reasons, and even for the wrong reasons.

What about in terms of staying relevant and dating? As I got older, I was once told I was too short to date someone who was my height or a little shorter. The other potential candidate indicated I had to be oh this much taller to get on their ride. Ride? Really? I was amused, not really. I was quick to reply, I had plenty of encyclopedias that I own that I could stand on. Ha! That did not work, but the potential liked my sass. Eventually, I ended up reversing the logic and returned the favor that future potential candidates had, and used the logic that they have to be this short to get on my ride. They were just as amused. Touché!

Moving on, how does one continue to stay relevant? I look for sayings that have been tested and proven successful through the ages.

"A penny for your thoughts." That is an interesting saying. When there is conflict in the home or between friends, sometimes a simple question after the flurry of discontent might seem relevant.

When one is lost either as a child or adult, and a parent, friend or another like yourself sees turmoil, asking that question, "A penny for your thoughts" might help them open up about what is bothering them.

Mind you, one might not be able to resolve the problem, but at least you are there to be of some comfort. Staring out a window and pondering life might help you ground yourself and realize if you are relevant or not. Thinking if you are good enough is not a question but a feeling.

Being a good listener is just as important as being a good problem solver. The hard part is knowing which to be when the time is right, or even when the timing is wrong.

Wisdom can come to you when you are happy where you are, and if this were the last day, you have or had no regrets, and not much else left to do except enjoy the moments. Your relevance of being you and your place in the universe can be at one.

Another idea I had a long time ago about being okay when relevance is being found is that your circle of control and your circle of concern are or are not the same size. If your circle of concern is larger than your circle of control, you are frustrated, and you are happier when quite the opposite; when your circle of control is larger than your circle of concern. Alas, I relax a moment for one to ponder.

Just realize you were perfect when you were born and through life you will mess a few things up and mess up a few relationships yet remember at the end, you will return to being perfect once again – life has a way of auto-correction in everyone's life one way or another.

In the process of moving to the end of your mortality, it is important to remain young at heart, young in your thinking, and thankful of the generation replacing you. Classics like your car, your clothes, and your games and reading material will be of interest to the next generation for some. Be sure to hand me down your relics and share the value you had in them. Tell your story like those of days gone past and have the next generation remember your stories and they somehow will find a way to carry those stories on to the next generation.

Stay Relevant by looking again at the macro and microscopic view of all things. Get a piece of paper out and jot down those ideas that you have running around in your head. Use a pencil to be a little old school and doodle something on the edge to make it your own. Then look through your folder of ideas and inventions and find a good place to put this latest piece of paper.

…more to come…

Chapter 9 – Putting it all Together

How does one tidy up their baggage and belongings before the end of your life? Does one really care what they leave on for others and in what shape and condition? Does it really matter?

I believe it does matter that when one starts to wrap up their mortality and believe they have turn the corner, so to speak. In terms of golfing, the first 9 was pretty good, and on the back 9 of their 18-hole life of golf, they start to see their friends and family vanish and are no longer part of their daily conversation, aside from prayers and sharing great stories and memories with those still alive on this planet.

So, I have to practice what I preach. The next paragraph belongs at the beginning of the book, as does so many other great lines of thinking.

Moral of the Story. Live life lightly and in doing so blissfully.

Do you have children? If not, that is okay too. I am sure you might be like me and it's not for a lack of trying, just not trying hard enough to consider what might your progeny might look like and be like.

For others, for some are blessed to have a DNA legacy while others may have a DNA legacy and not know it. Still others might have a large family tree both above and below them, and all around themselves. That is good.

Let me tell you a secret, something you may have heard in one form or another, but still just as good.

There was a story I heard of a long time ago about someone being born at midnight in this hotel room. It's about life, when you are born, how you grow up and grow old and eventually die. Here is that story....

The room was empty, neat and simple. A bed, dresser, chair, mirror and lamp; it was all that was there. As they grew up to be in their twenties the clock moved to 6am and a few more things started to appear, some books on a bookshelf, some clothes on a clothes rack, and some drapes on the window. Their life continued on and when the clock struck 12 noon, about half the room was full of things, boxes of this and that, and it seemed to be a little cluttered. The person was able to move around but not as easily as earlier in the day. The clock moved past 3pm and a few more things appeared, some cobwebs appeared in the corners, the carpet started to get dusty and the person was in the late 50's when the clock struck 6pm. Life seemed good but the hotel room was really started to show no more room to add things. Nevertheless, the clock moved to 9pm and the person was starting to get tired, and they could not get around the room because of so much stuff in their way, and they did not have the strength and energy to move it. They could barely find the bed in order to take rest. It did not matter because by the time the clock struck 11pm the person was old and in their 90s and could not get up to get rid of the things they had. When the clock chimed 12 midnight the person died and was gone. Instantly the room was empty and like it was 24 hours prior, new, fresh and ready to start a new.

Interesting story, huh? Moral of the story? Don't waste your life collecting things, junk-junk-junk, and baggage. It clutters your ability to live freely. All that stuff is not yours anyhow. You just get to steward and tend to it for a little while anyhow.

Write the ending at the beginning.

Have you ever had to say all that you have had to say, and then summarize what you have learned in the end? In some case law, the head notes are for the judge or lawyer to know all about what they are going to read and know the ending before they read it. That sounds like cheating and skipping to the end of the story in a suspense novel, but I can assure you there is a good reason to start at the beginning with the ending. Try it.

Complex and subtle thoughts are the present future.

Use cliff notes whenever possible. If you don't know what cliff notes are, then your age is showing. Please feel free to resurrect them for yourself and how you approach life. We don't have enough time to hear all your rants and raves at the same time. The 1-minute egg timer is ticking and your five seconds are about up.

Random Notes:

- *opportunity abounds when there is major distraction*
- *law of attraction exists where there is imbalance*
- *game of chance and luck works when preparedness exists*
- *when things aren't working, move out and move on*
- *if your efforts are not being heard or understood, change your language, vocabulary, and dictionary*

WHAT'S MY VALUE ADD

Have you ever heard of a good timeline? A timeline that reveals how things could or should go versus how they really went. Consider in how you wrap up your life in one page or less. Here is my brief attempt. Please feel free to adapt this for your own life.

IDEAL LIFELINE

Born, find your faith, travel, graduate from some school(s)

Work, get married, 2+ children, write books, invent things, travel

Retire, children married, grandbabies exist, travel

Die, afterlife in your heaven, legacy lives on

REALITY SETS IN LIFELINE

Born, never find your faith, don't graduate, never travel

Don't work, never marry or married 2+ times, no children

No retirement, outlive your children, never travel, never write a book

Die, no legacy, no afterlife

If you were to go back and do it all over again, would you, and if you did, would you change anything?

In closing, let's talk about the book cover for a moment. Notice anything? There are a few things, numerically and symbolically going on. 1, 2, 3, 7 – one sun, one ocean, one boat, one face, one lighthouse, one inlet or bay, two ducks, three crosses, seven waves, and seven trees.

In 2005, I sketched this for a PhD philosophy course. ~andy

Chapter 10 – Epilogue

The Coup de Gras! Write the ending at the beginning.

Have you ever had to say all that you have had to say, and then summarize what you have learned in the end? In some case law, the head notes are for the judge or lawyer to know all about what they are going to read and know the ending before they read it. That sounds like cheating and skipping to the end of the story in a suspense novel, but I can assure you there is a good reason to start the beginning with the ending. Try it all the time if you can.

Ironically, what makes us more in common is our ability to accept our differences and abilities without the propensity of greed and pride. When you do something - consider your motivation.

Oh, by the way, the political system is chaos. We should just be the American Party since we are all American; not democratic nor republican, nor green, nor independent, nor whatever. Well, maybe dependent on being independent. Solve the issues continuously like we do in business at great speed at with the least expense, and spend all our energy on that, and not on remaining at difference and opposite of each other. Many of my congress people need to learn to stop playing games with each other and the public and just shut up and do their job, and blabbing all the time is not it.

What will be on your headstone that sums of your life? Will there be some sort of poetry that you like that represents your beginning, middle and end? The Rule of Three applies to each and every aspect of your life; what I was, what I am, and what I will be.

…more to come…even if this is The End.